I0478813

Michel Simonidy

Edited by Lacey Belinda Smith

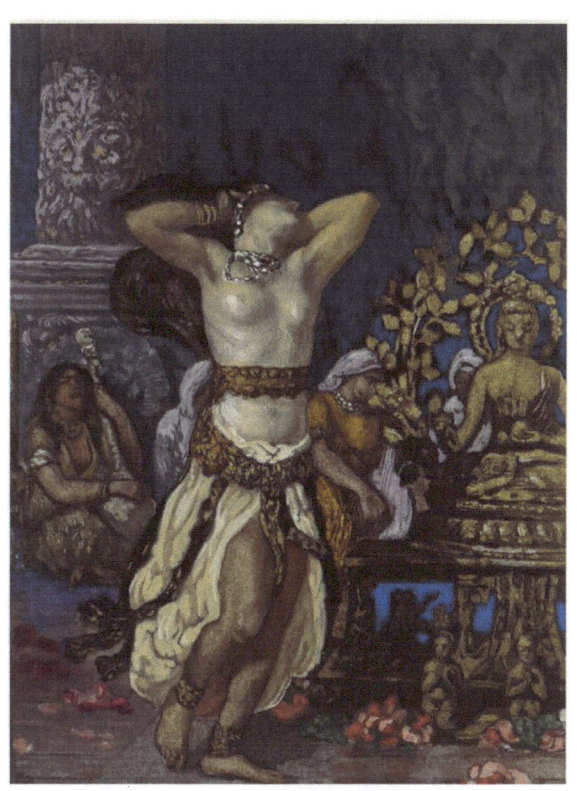

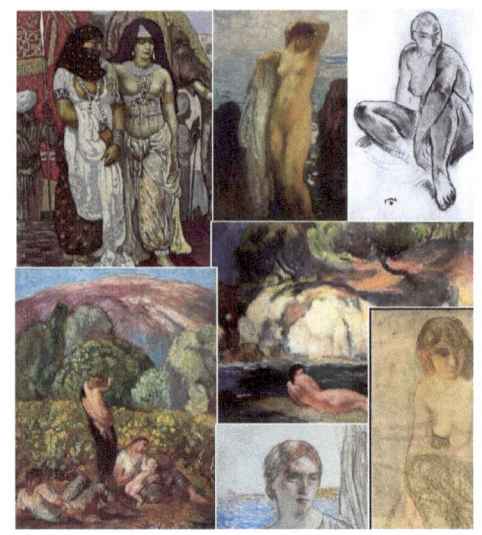

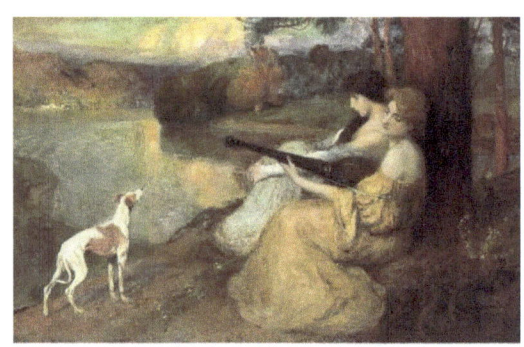

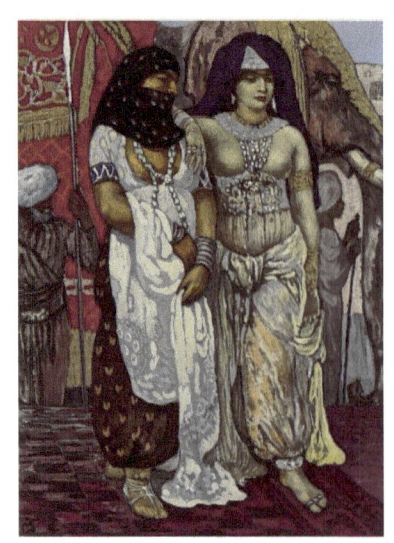

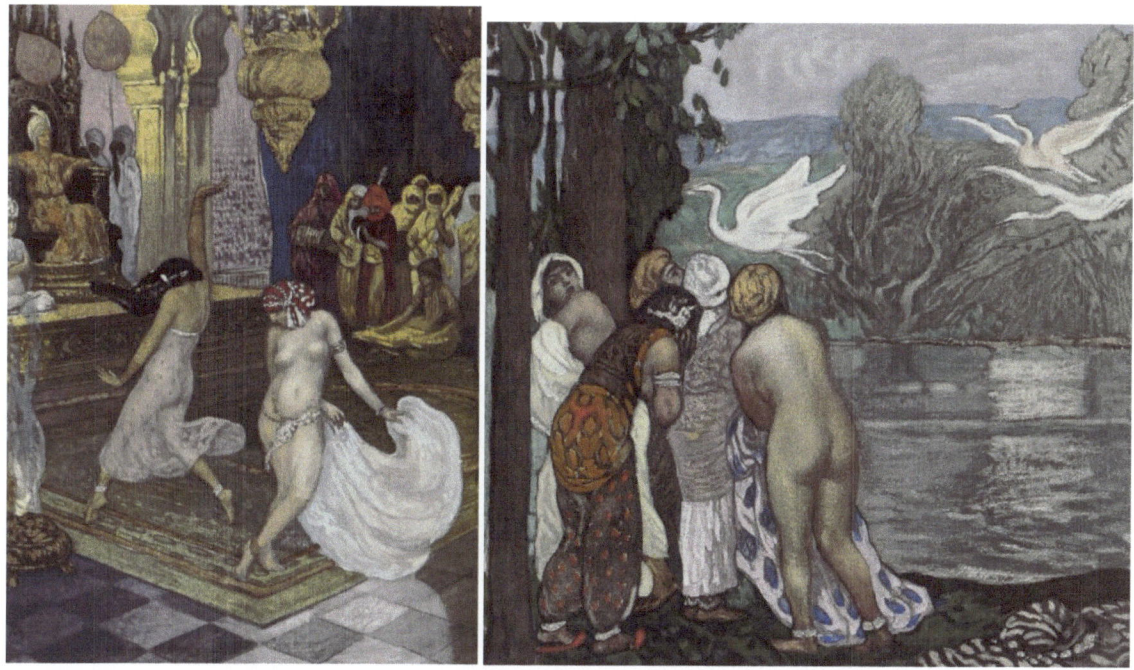

Illustrator and painter Michel Simonidy was from a Greek family but; he was born in Bucharest, Romania. He studied and lived much of his life in France. Michel Simonidy was a student of Leon Bonnat, Gabriel Ferrier, and Fernand Humbert. During his lifetime, he was well known for his still life paintings, portraits, symbolist images, allegorical works, historical scenes, figures, nudes, posters, landscapes, and marine scenes. He worked in oil, pastel, watercolor, and gouache. His style was that of Art Nouveau, and is characterized by the use of bold colors, blurred edges and fantasy-like scenes.

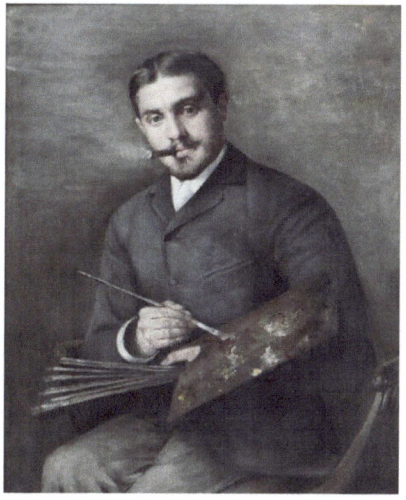

Michel Simonidy by Constantin Pascali

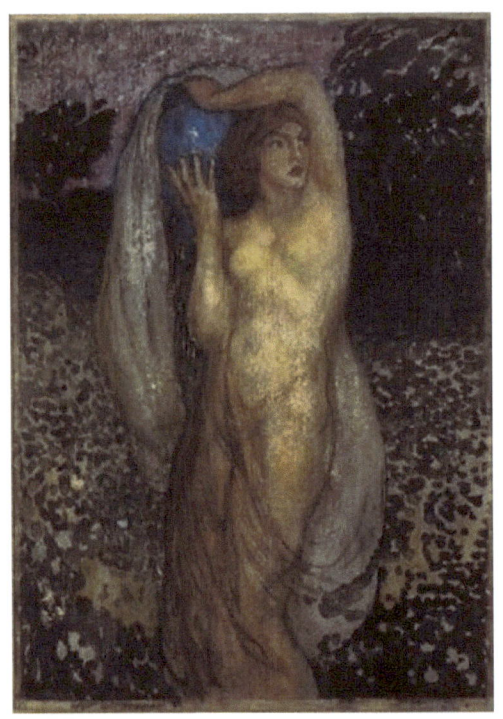

Baigneuse de nui--1895

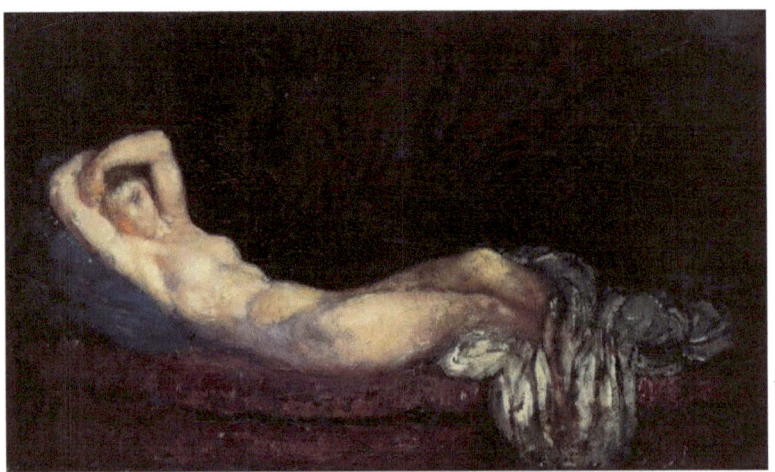

Femme nue allongée

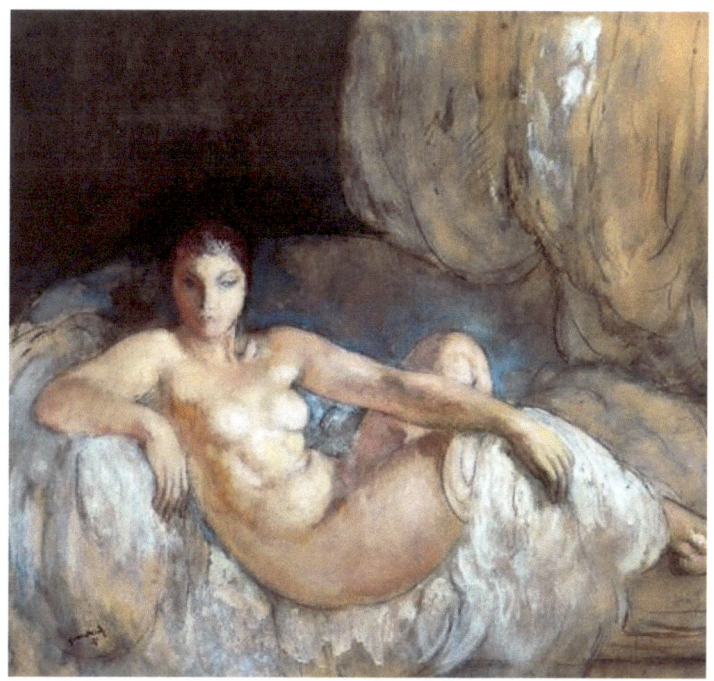

Desnudo--1927

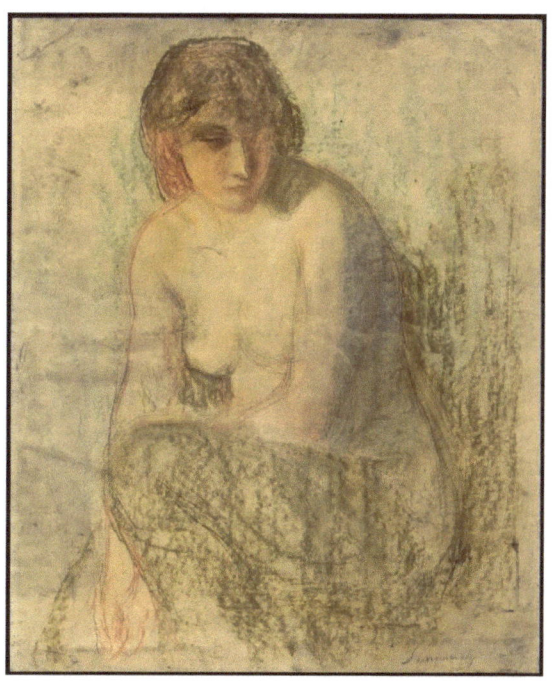

Femme nue penchee en avant

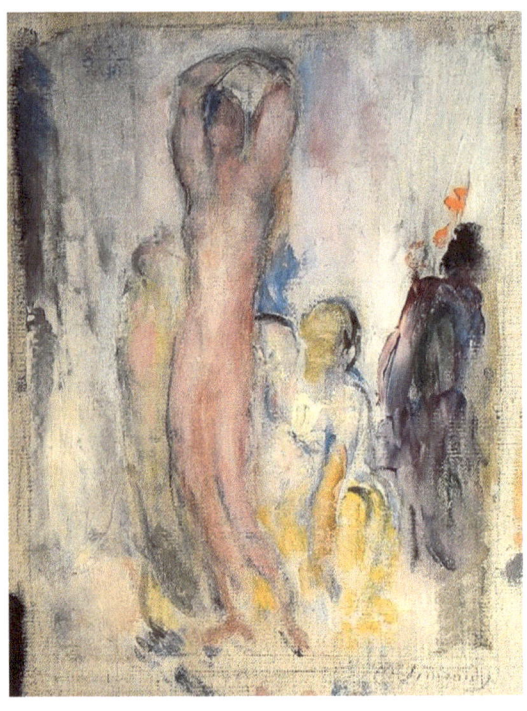

Delicate etude symboliste d une femme nue debout et ses servantes

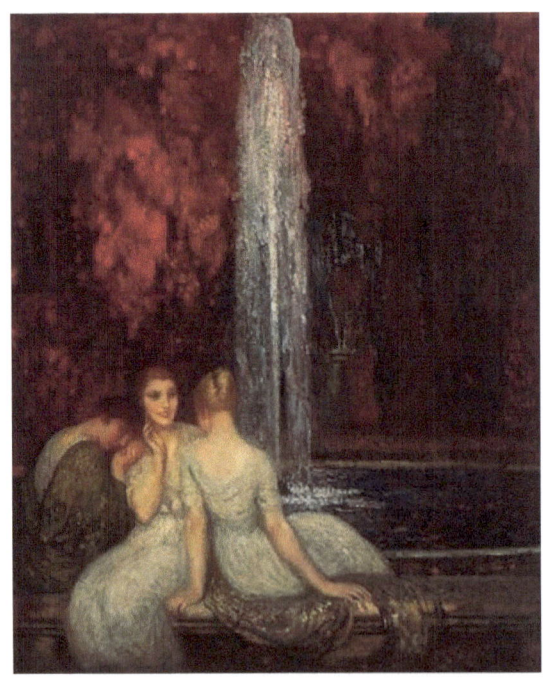

Confidenţe, 1905–1910

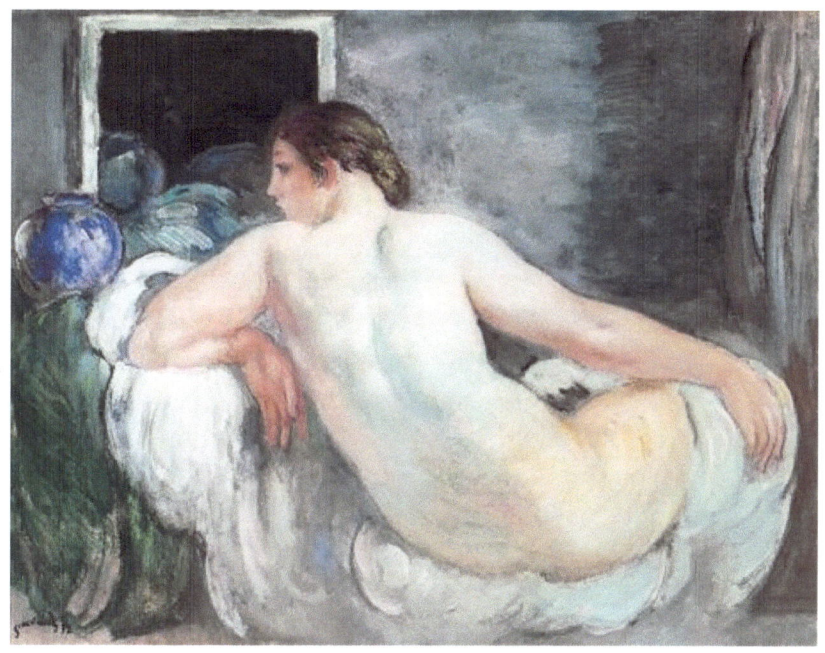

Intimitate

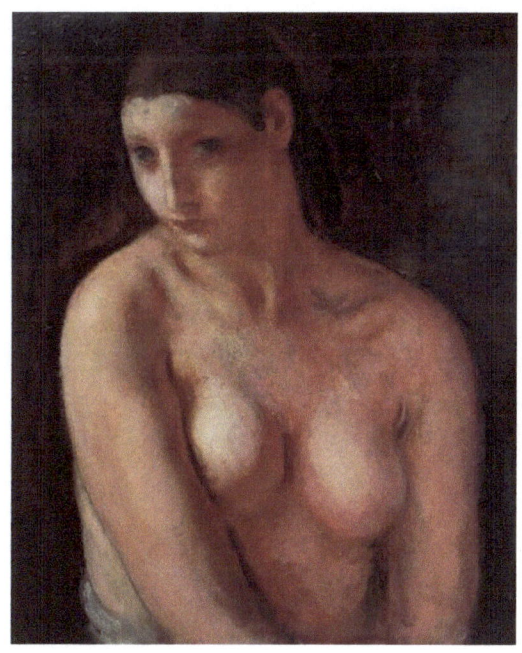

Bust De Jeune Fille--1925

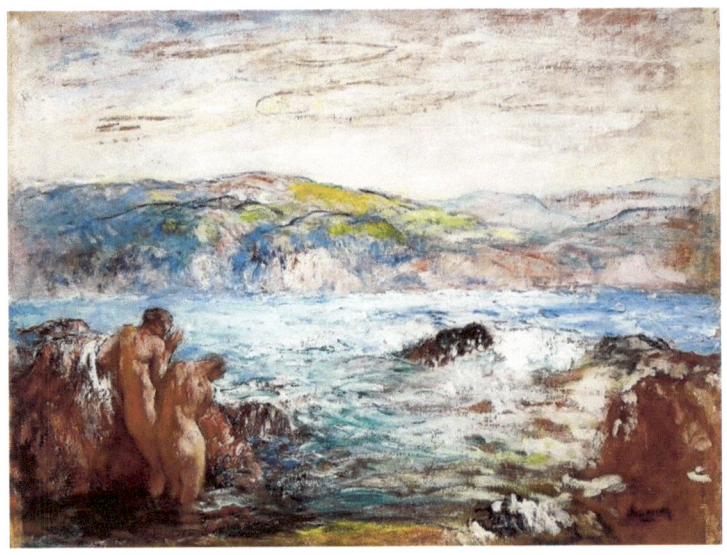

Marine Landscape--1900

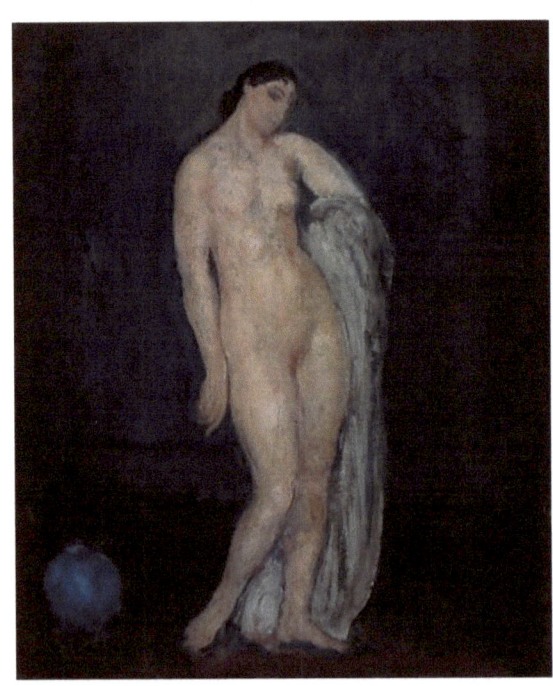

Nude With Blue Vase--1925

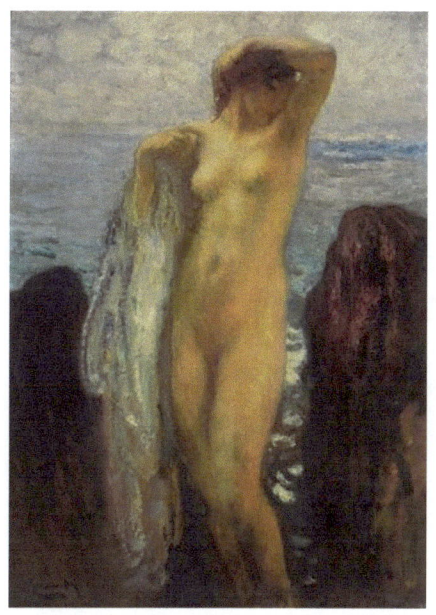

Desnudo en las rocas

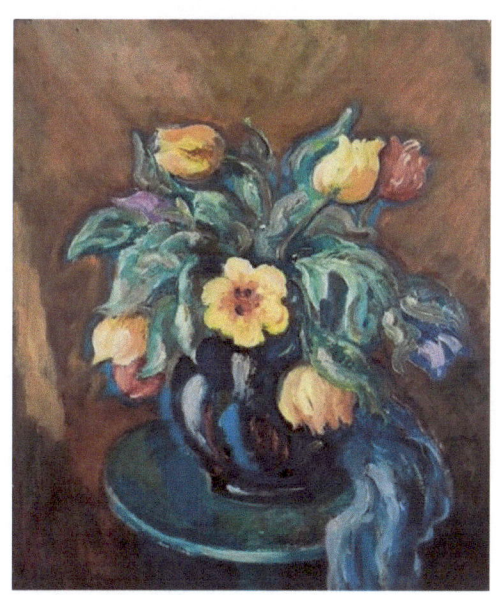

Flowers

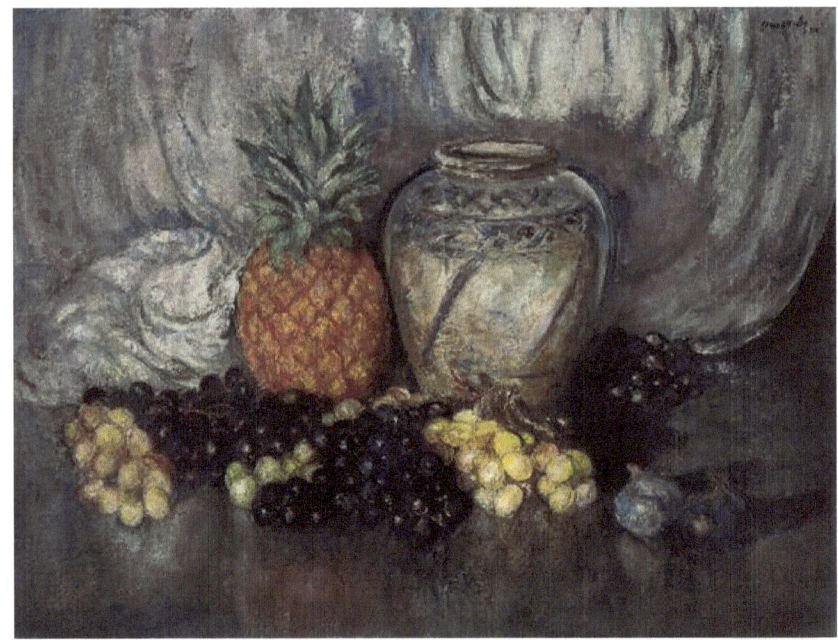

Bodegón

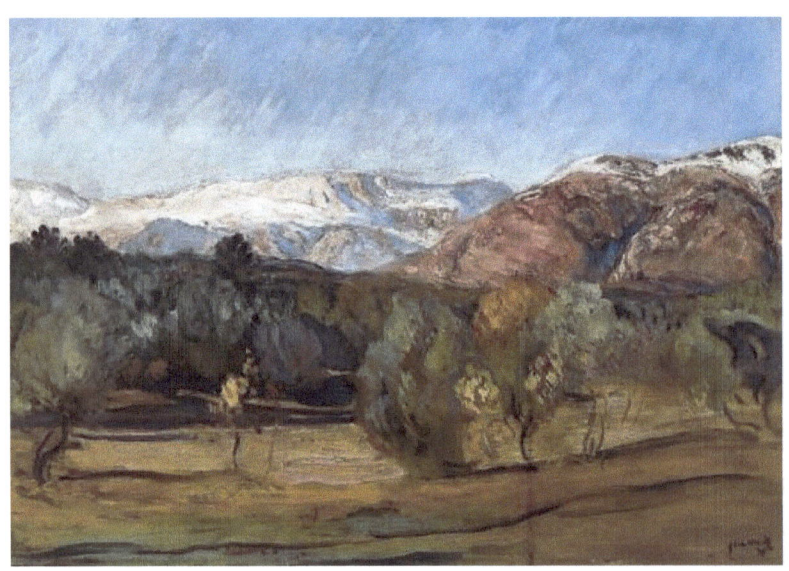

Paysage dans les Alpes Maritimes

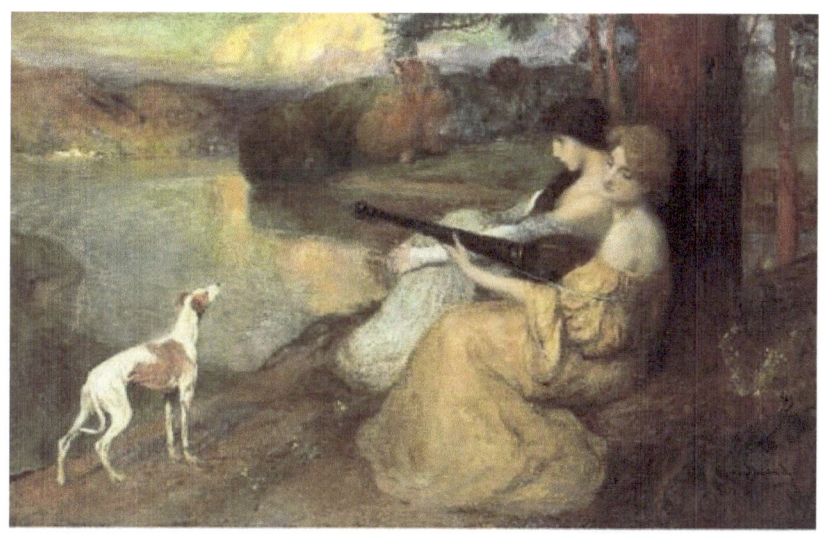

Harmonie Du Soir--1905

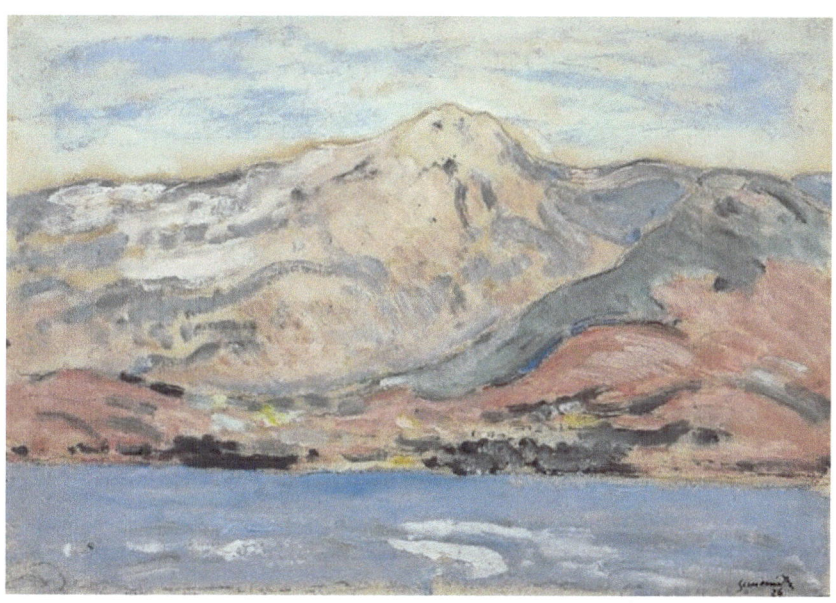

Peloponnese

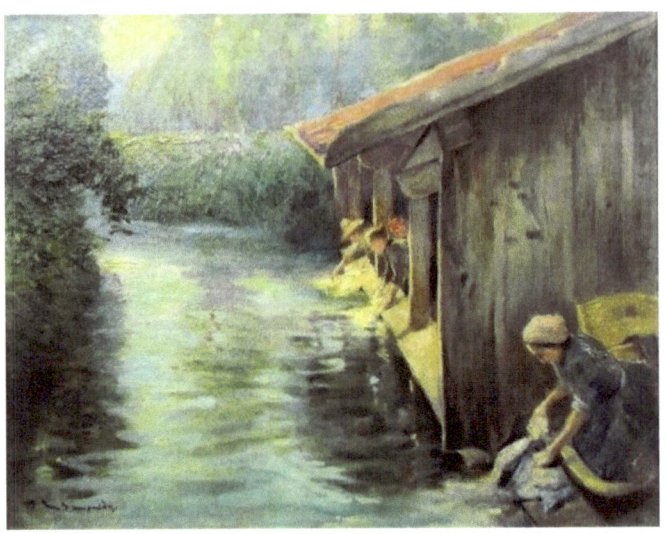

Washing the Laundry at the River--1895

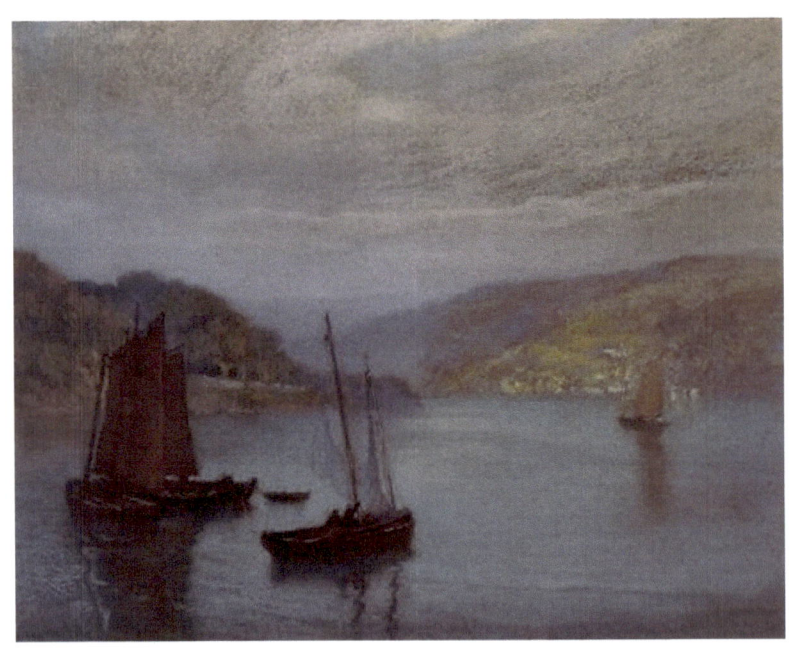

Voiliers au mouillage, Bretagne

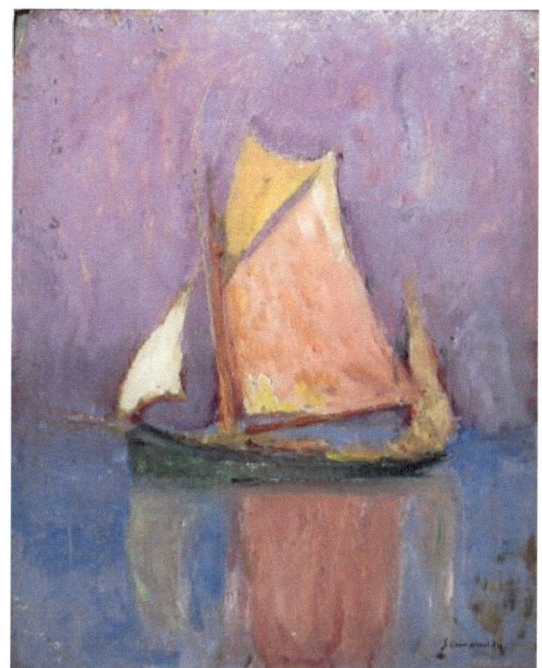

Iolă

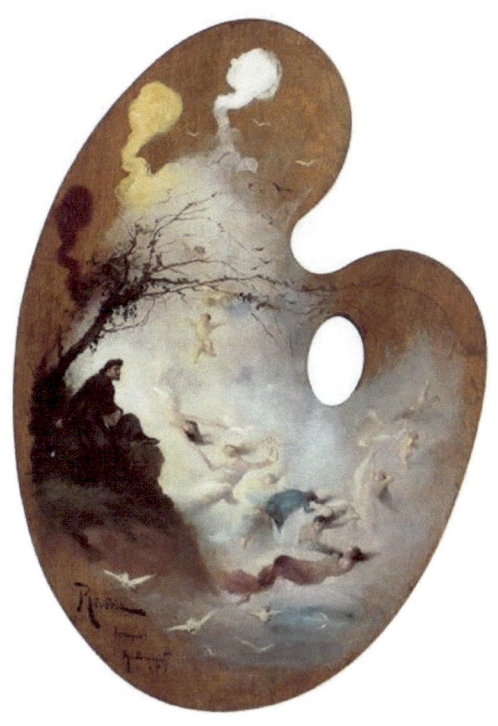

Reverie (The Dream Of The Monk)-- 1891

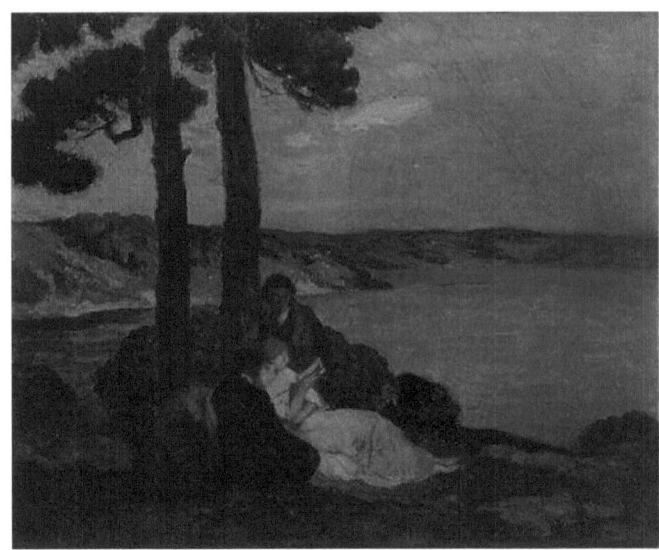

La lecture--1910

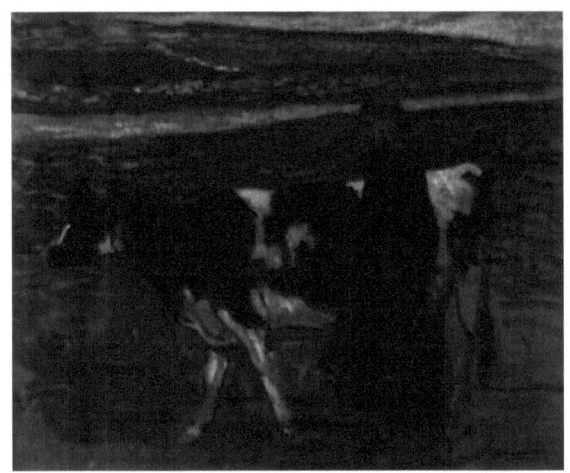

Fille de pêcheur à Quiberon gardant une vache--1916

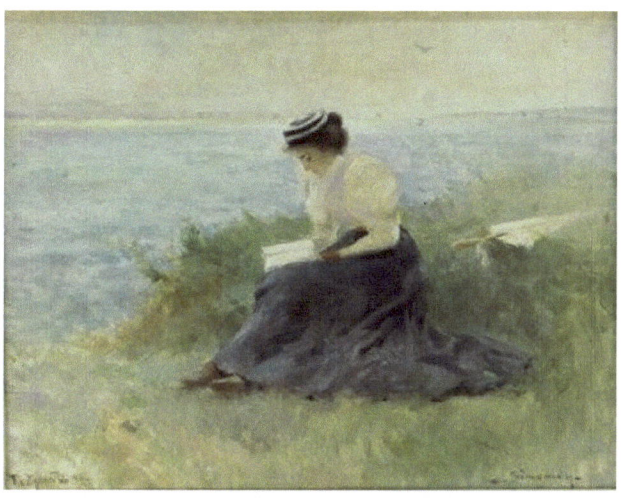

Femeie Pe Malul Mării

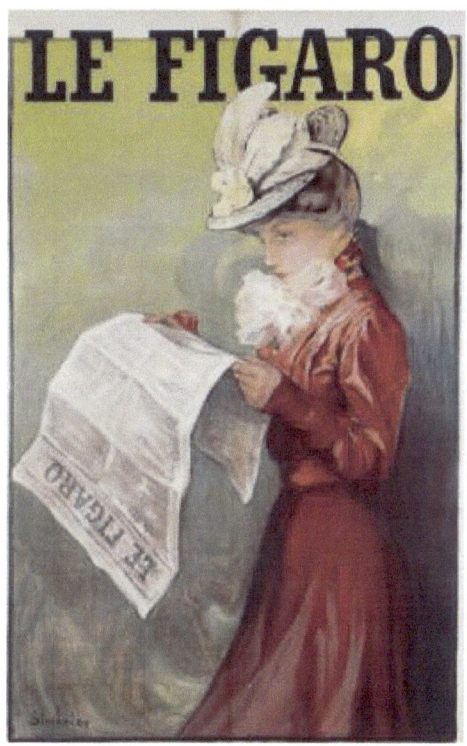

Le Figaro Newspaper

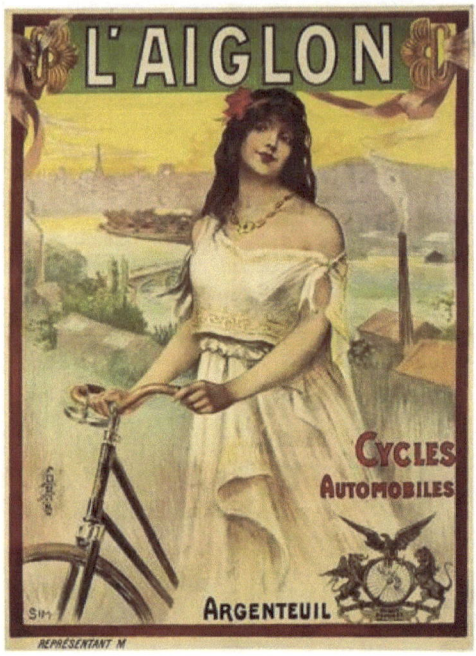

L'aiglon Cycles Automobiles

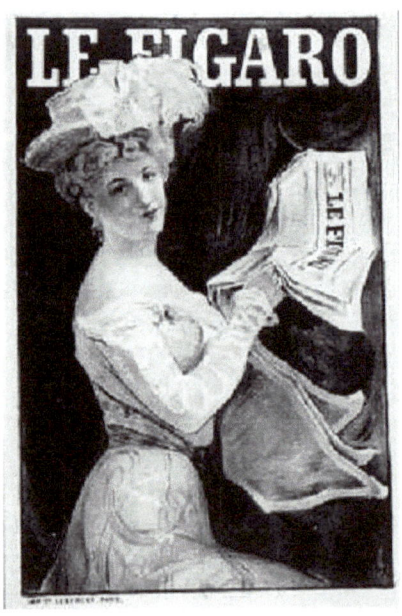

Le Figaro-- 1900

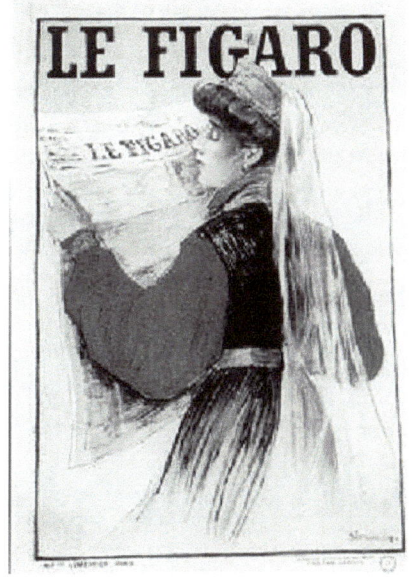

Le Figaro--1900

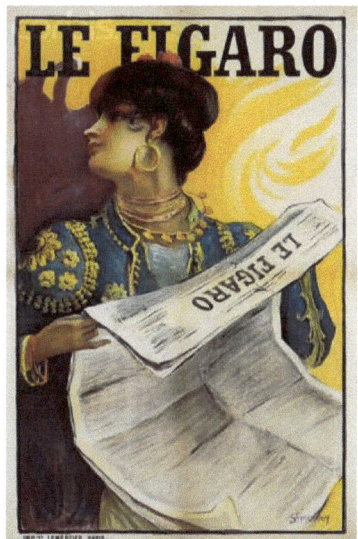

Le Figaro--1900

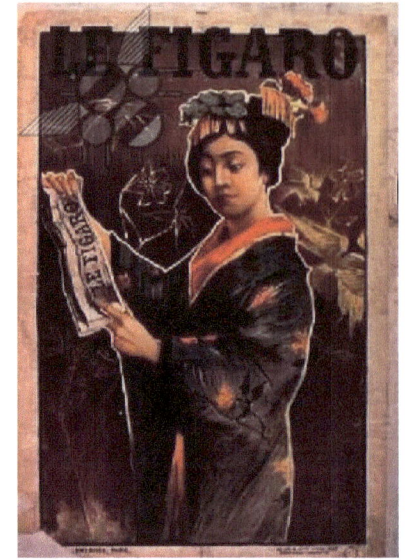

Le Figaro--1900

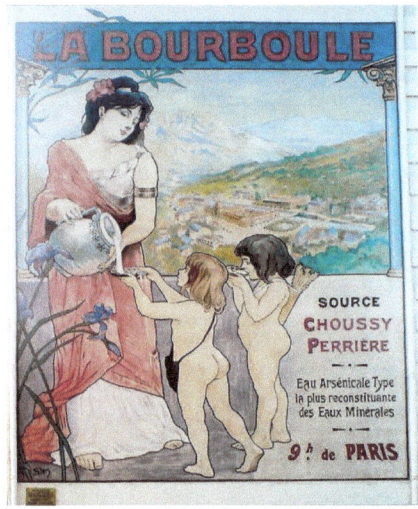

Affiche La Bourboule

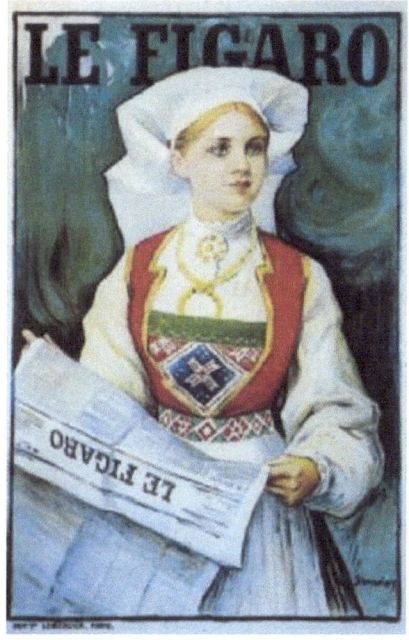

Le Figaro--1900

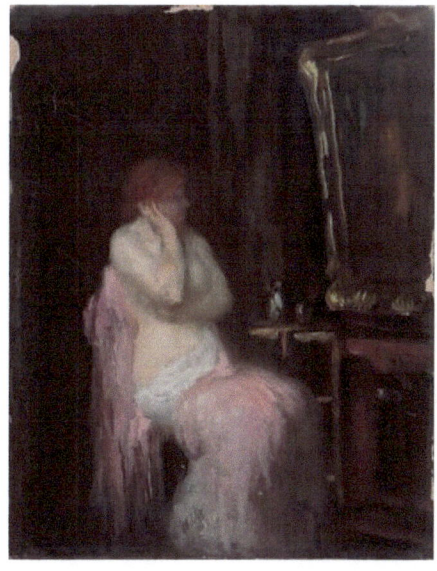

Femme devant un miroir

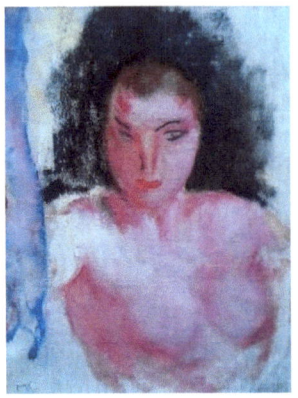

Female Nude

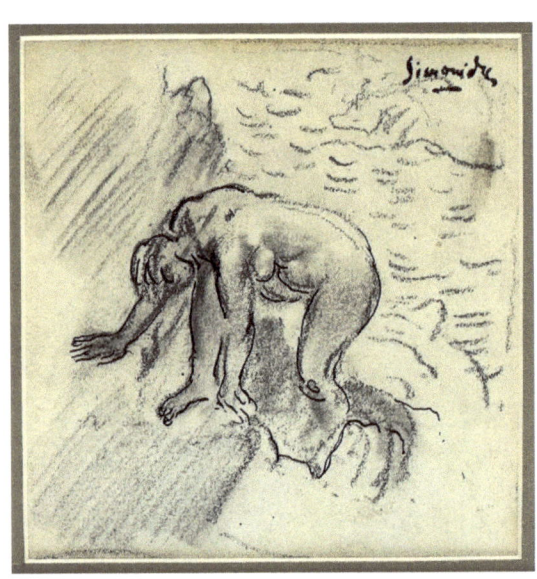

Sea foam--ink on paper

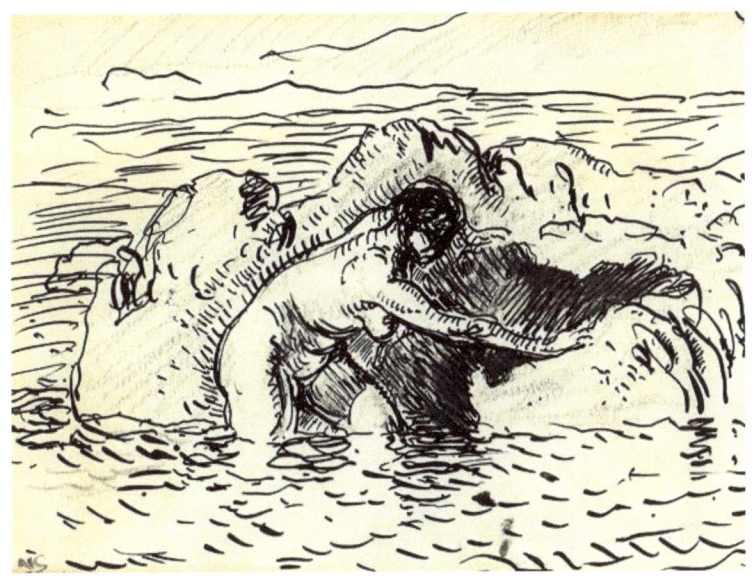

Baigneuză-- ink on paper

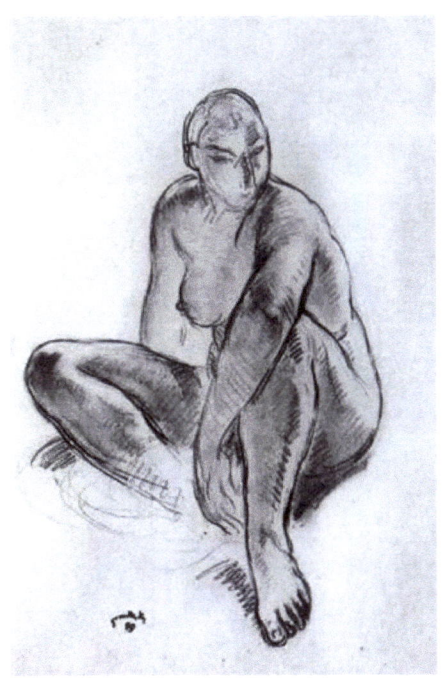

Femme assise--1929--charcoal

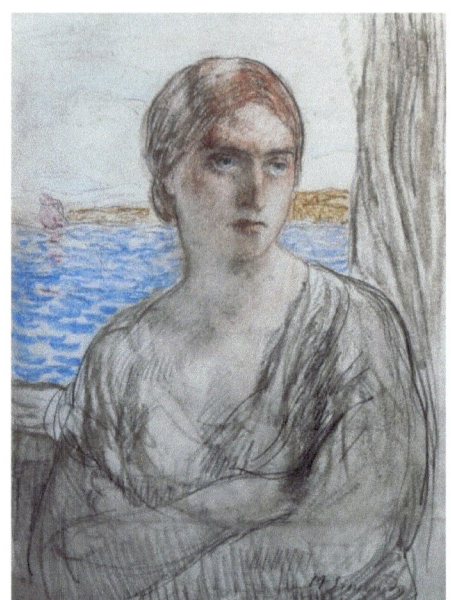

Devant la fenêtre--charcoal and pencil

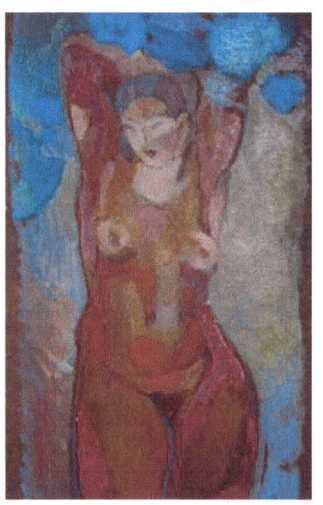

Nude

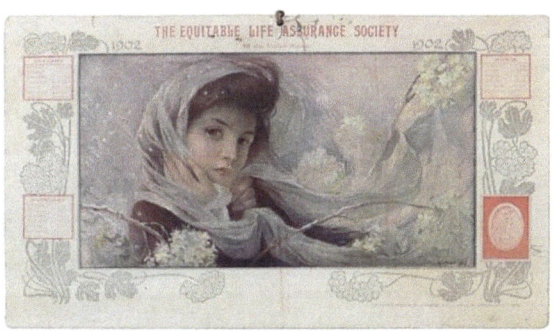

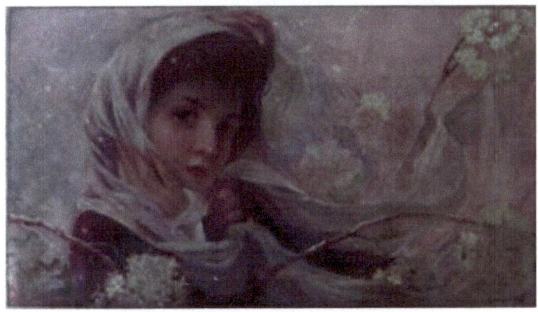

The equitable life assurance society (calendar w/4 works)--1902

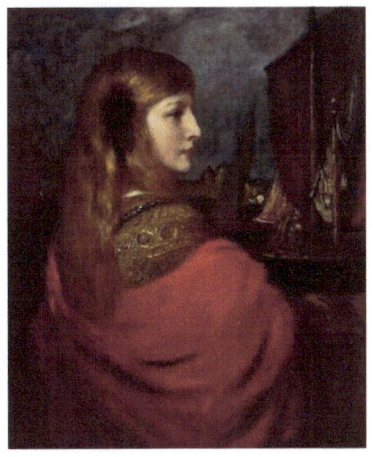

A fair Venetian

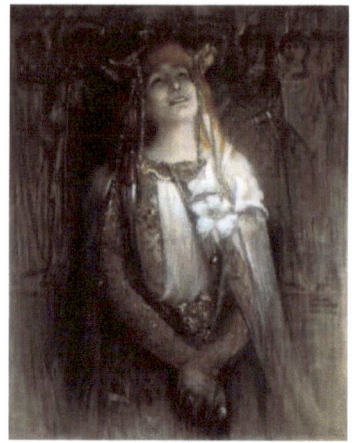

Sarah Bernhardt In Teodora Bizanțului--1903

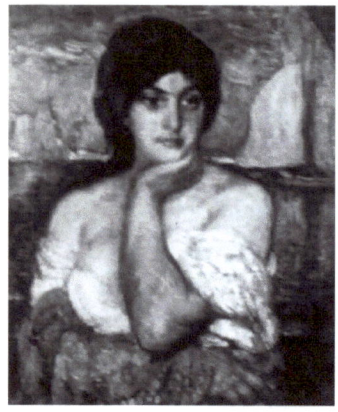

La belle Vénitienne

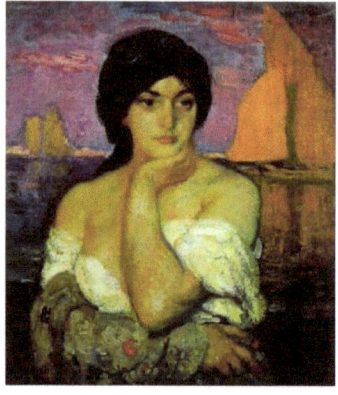

Porträt einer jungen Frau vor einer Hafenlandschaft

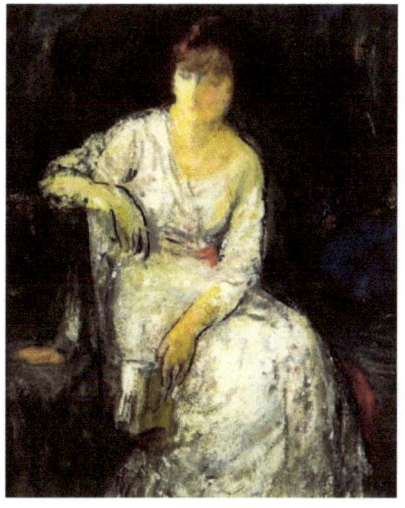

Liseuse

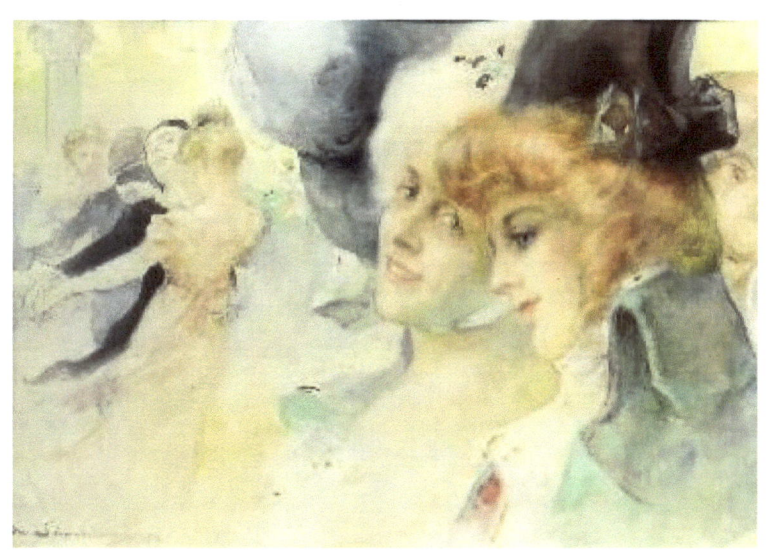

The Ball--1899

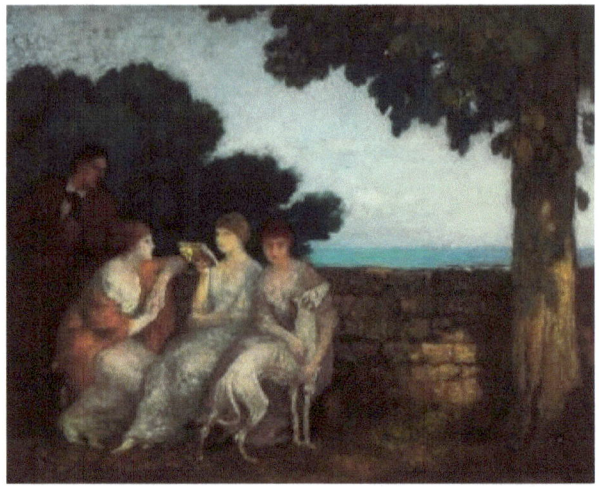

Three Maidens in Garden with Dog and Standing Gentleman--1905

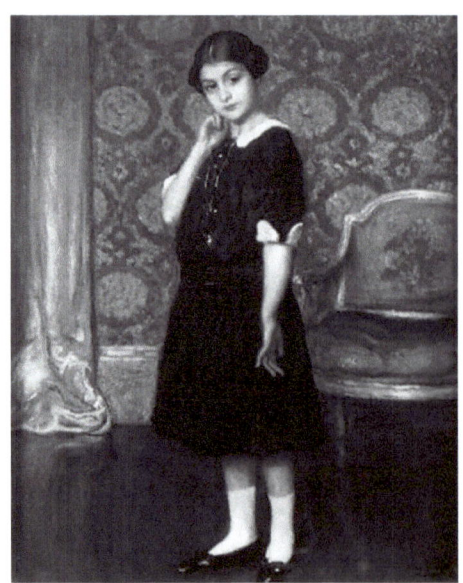

La robe bleue--1913

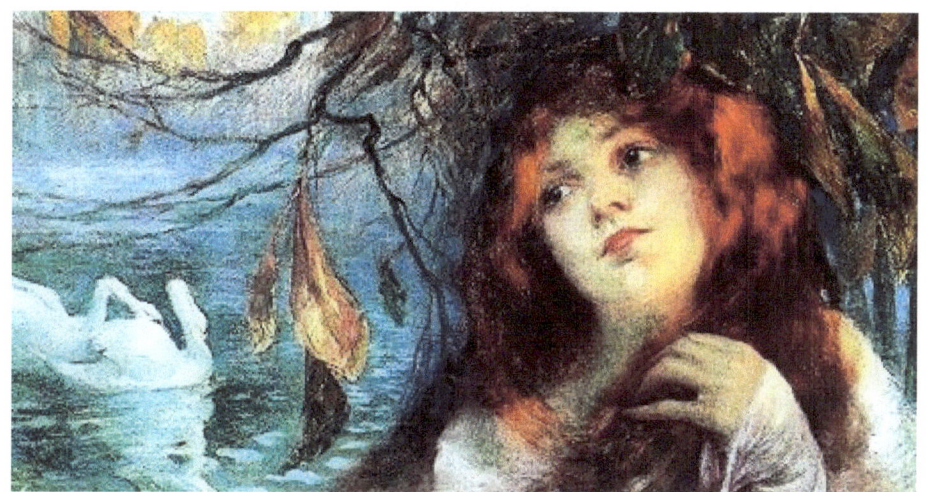

Reverie Au Bord Du Lac

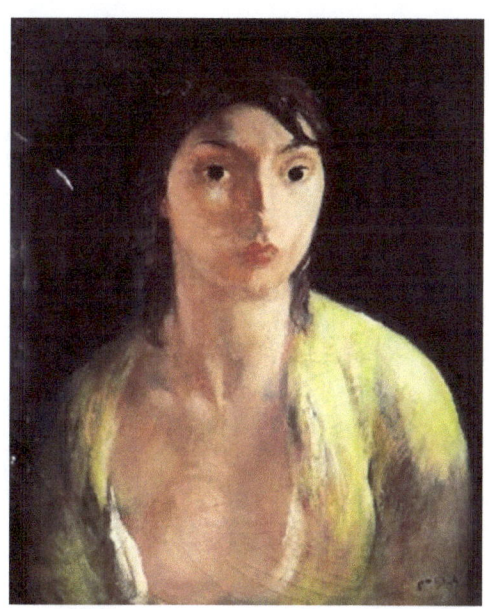

Portrait Of A Woman

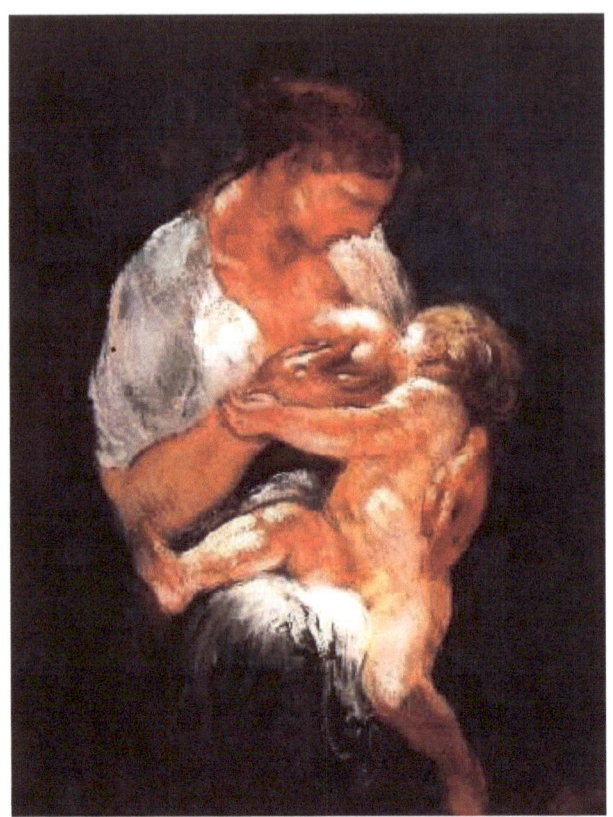

Mother And Child

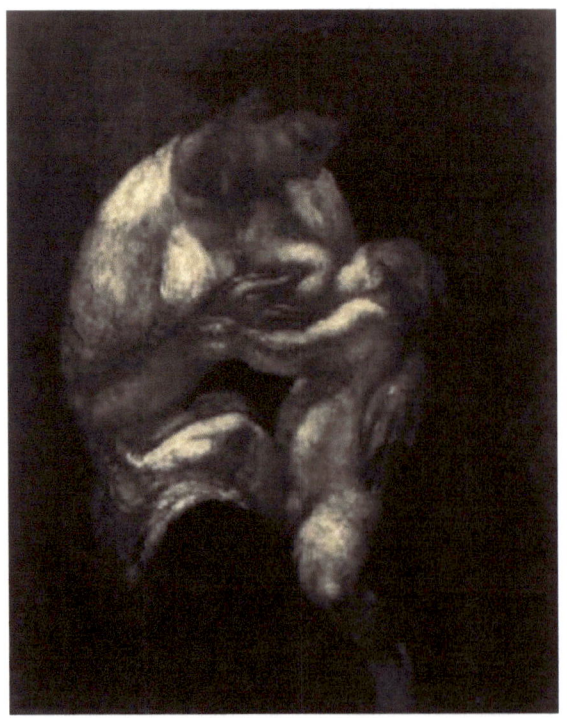

Maternité

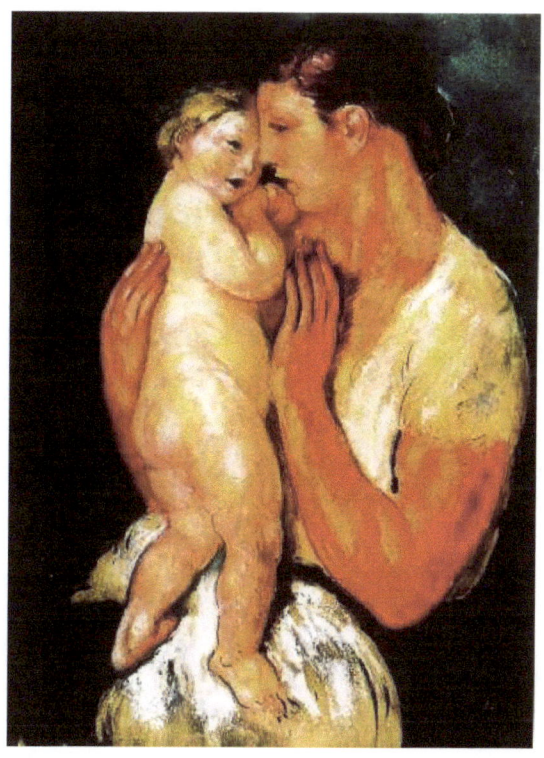

Maternitate--1928

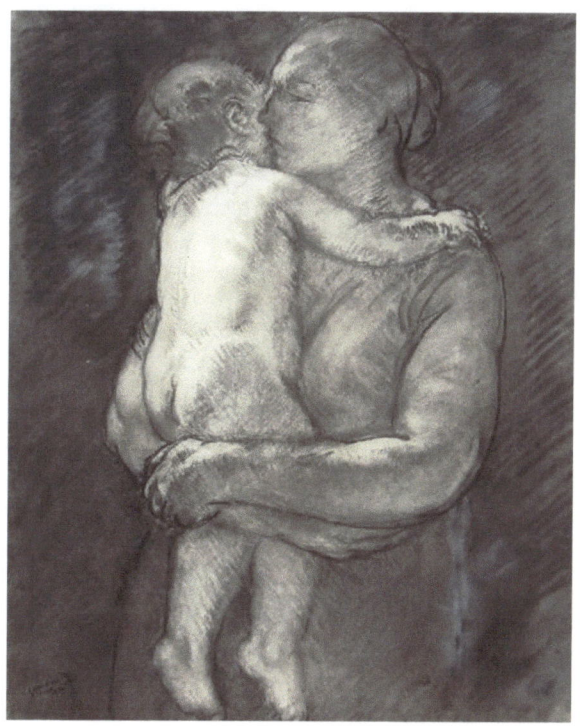

Maternité

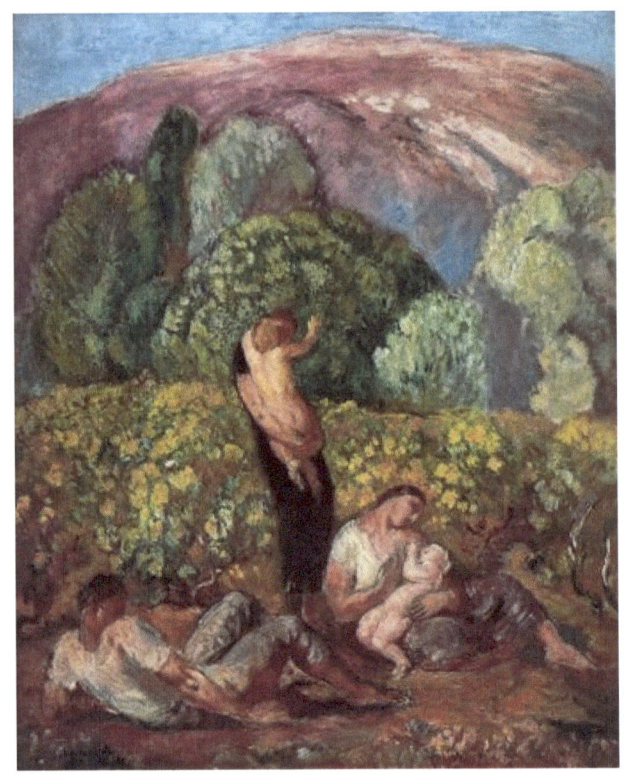

Maternitate (ciclu "Pastorala")--1928

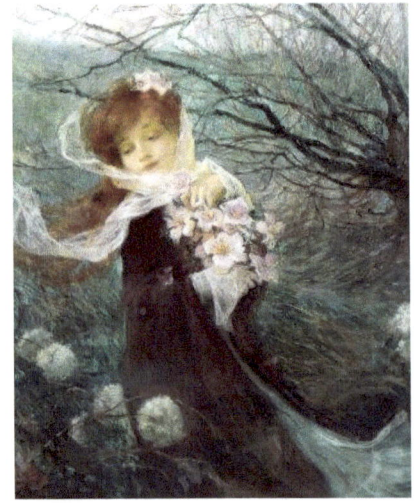

Winter Perfume--1902

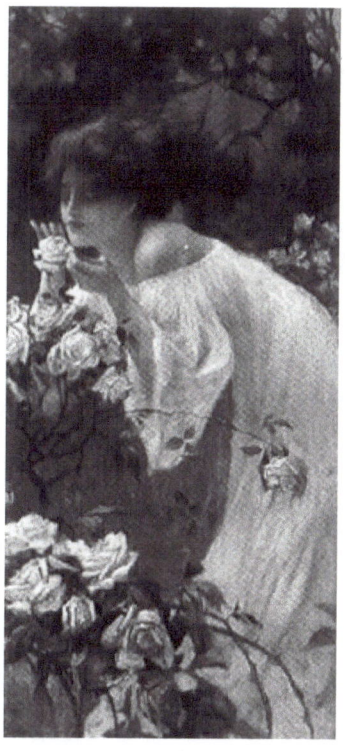

Summer--1901

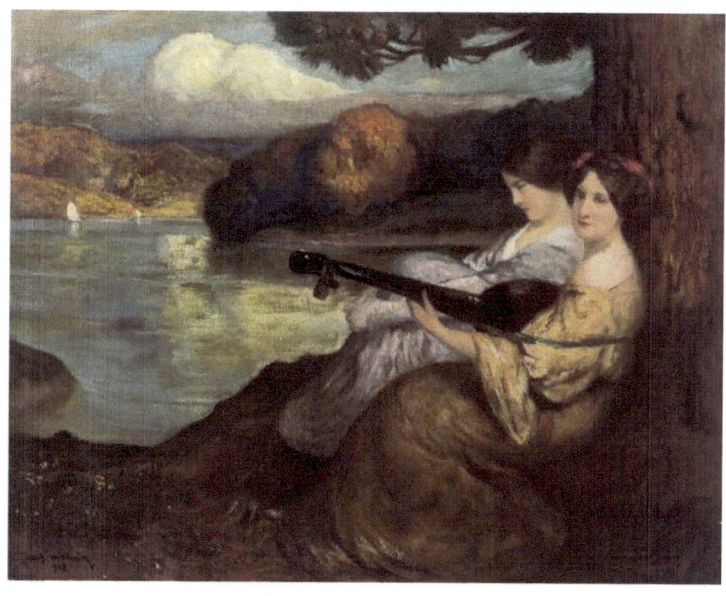

Autumn Song--1908

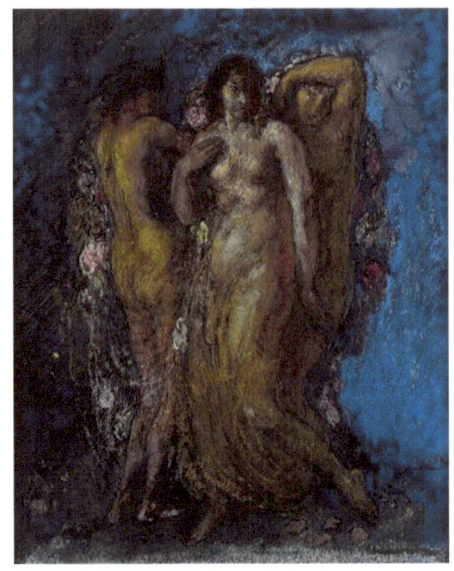

The Three Graces, Pastel

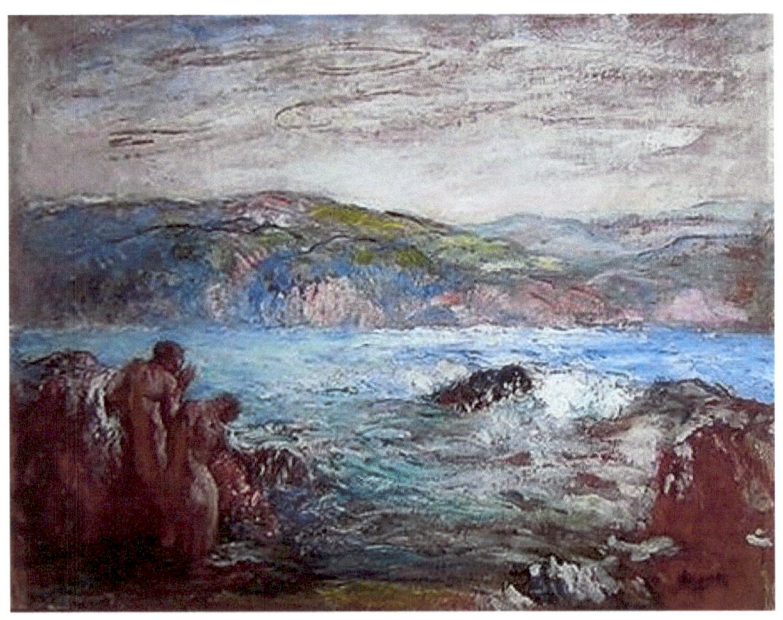

Swimming

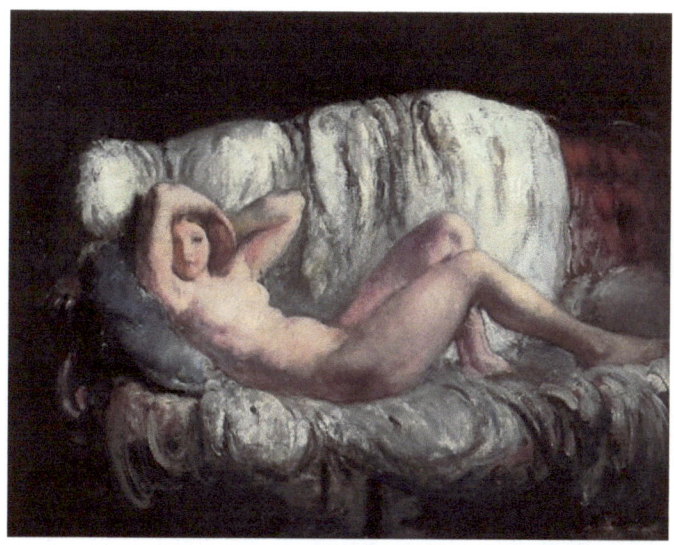

Frumusețe

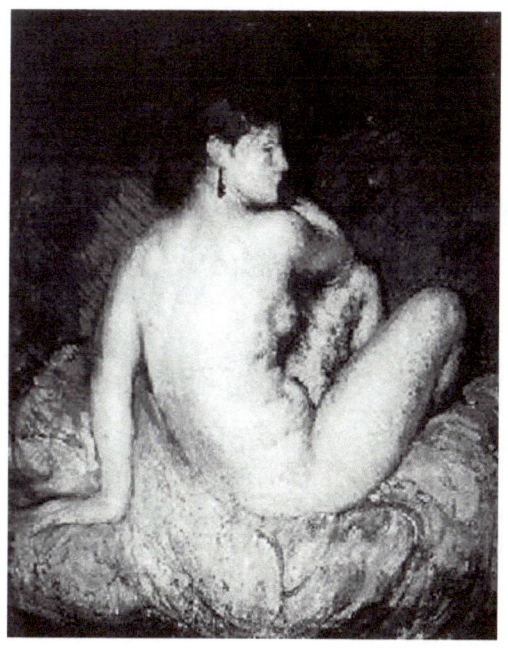

A beauty in the waiting

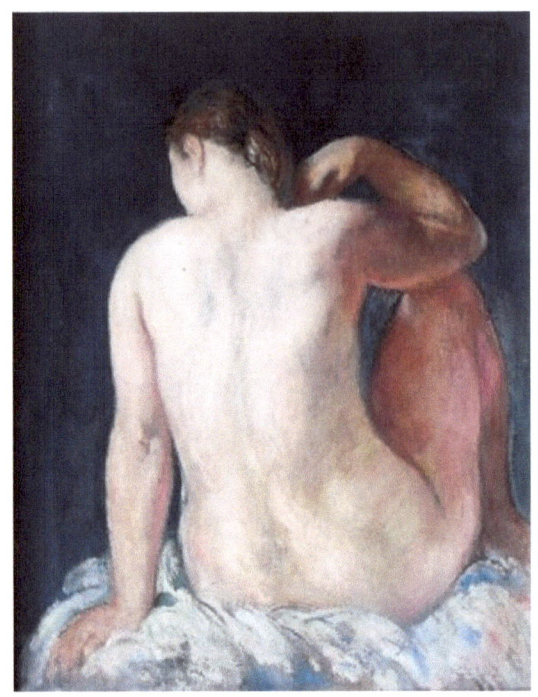

Nu de dos-- 1929

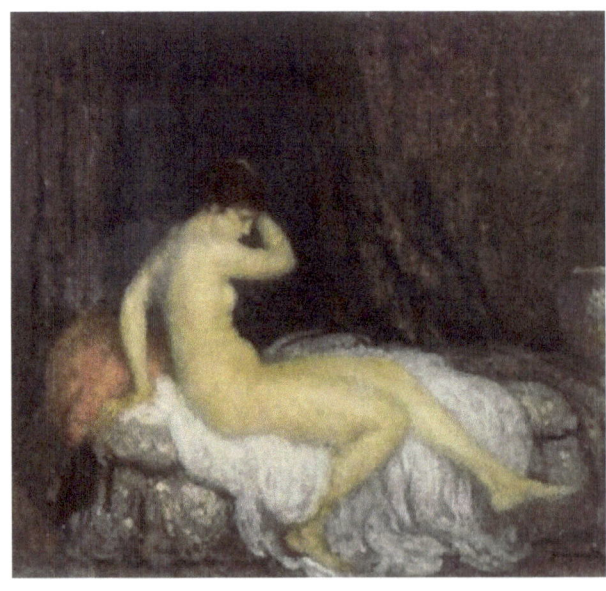

Femme au sofa

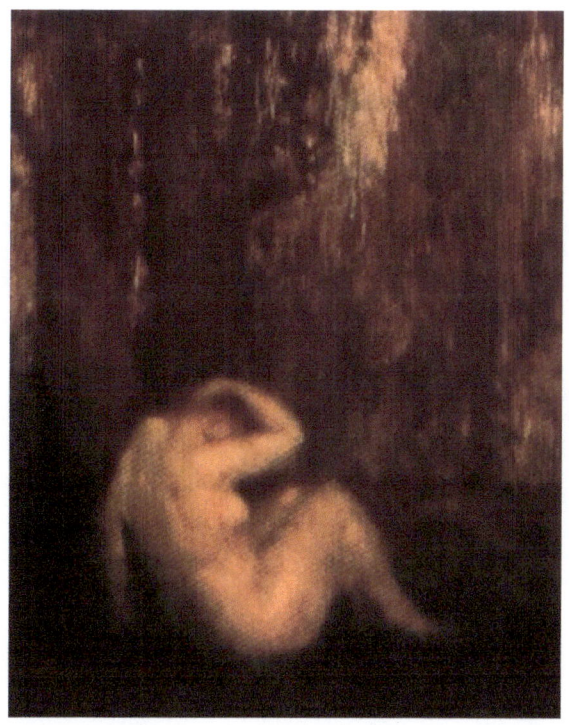

Nu assis dans un sous-bois

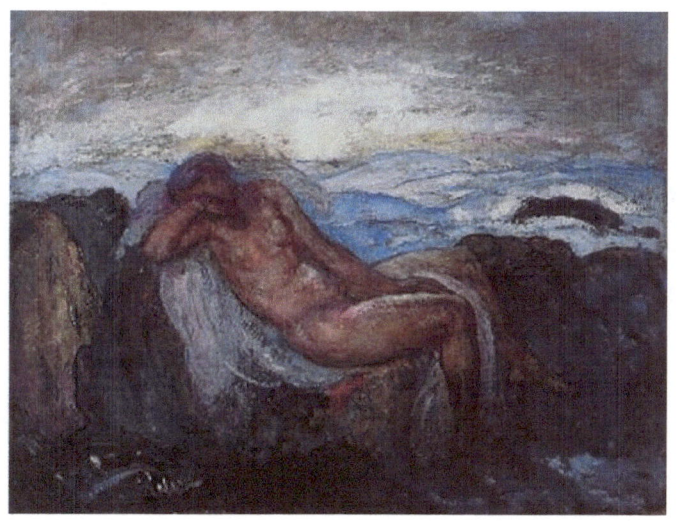

Baigneuse aux rochers--1922

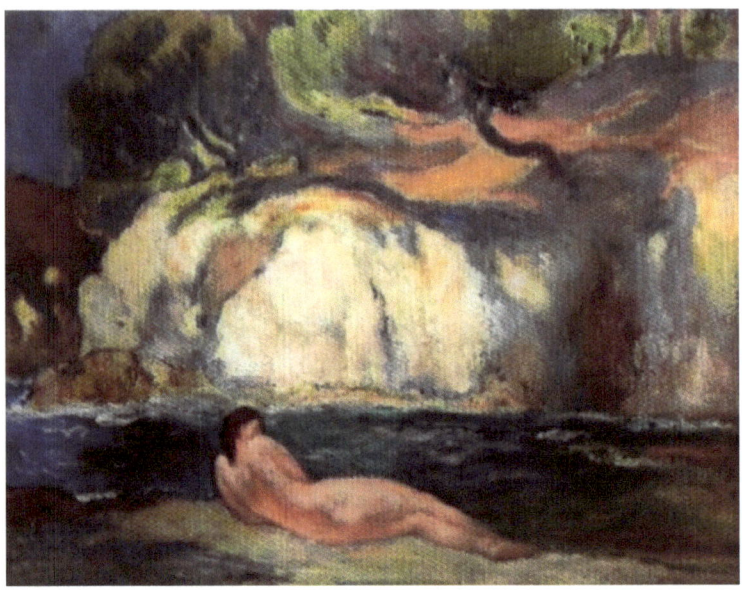

Baigneuse--1927

Histoire de Minoutchehr: Selon le Livre des Rois.– 1919 is the fifth volume of the great poetic Persian saga--*Shahnameh* ("Book of Kings"), composed by the poet Aboul Kasim Firdousi. It tells It tells the story of the Persian Empire from the creation of the world until the Islamic conquest in the 7th century. The *Shahnameh* is the world's longest epic poem created by a single poet. It was translated in french by Jules Mohl and Illustrated by Michel Simonidy

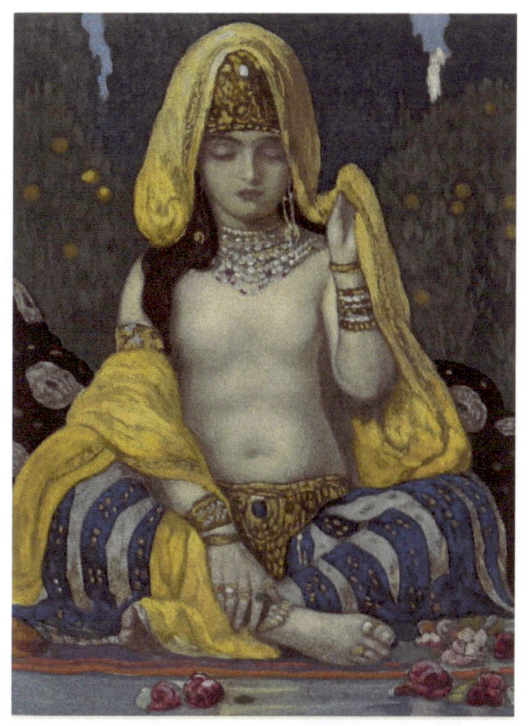

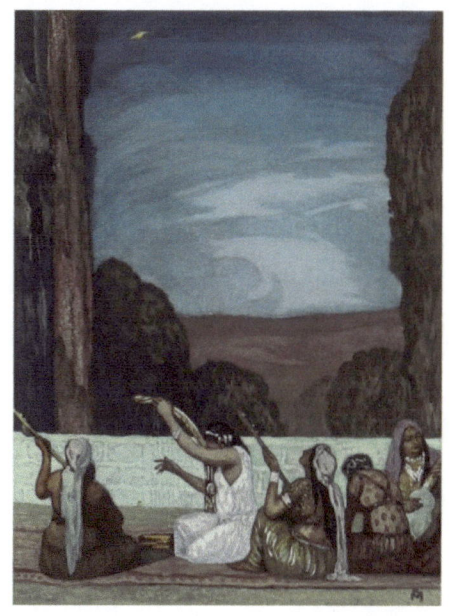

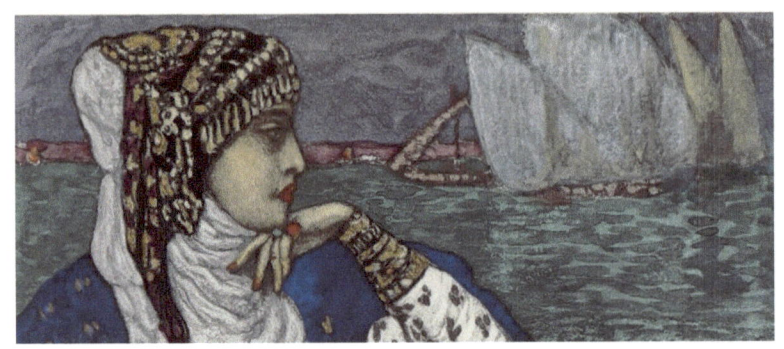

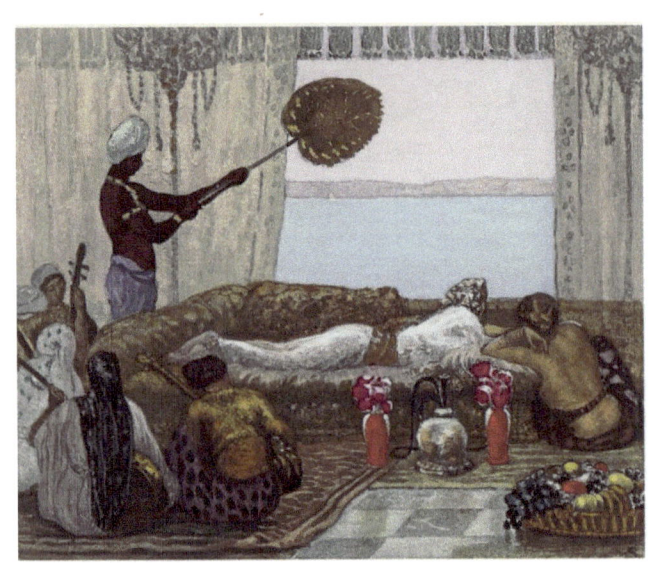

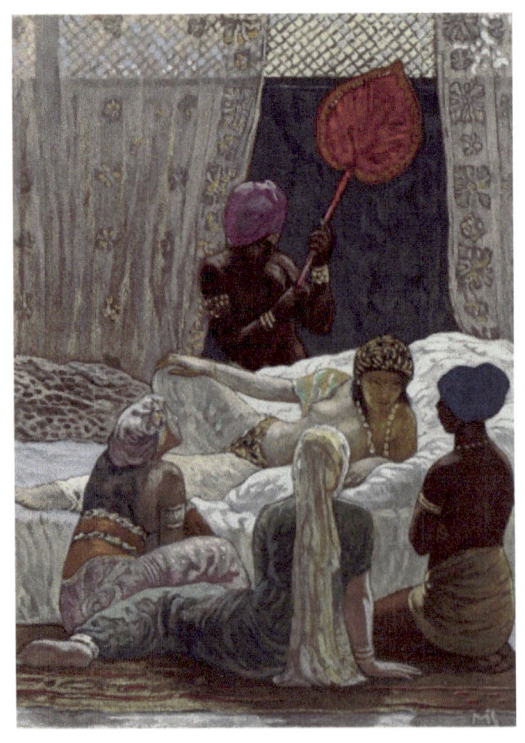

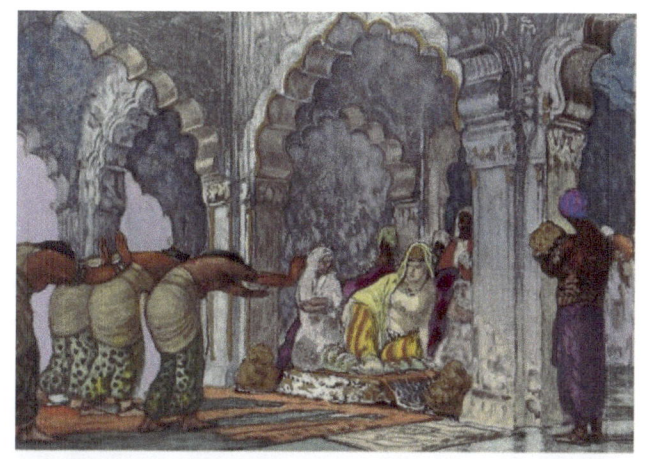

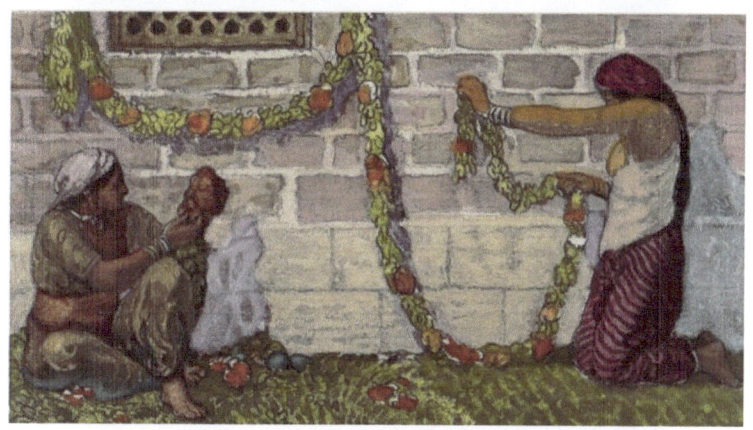

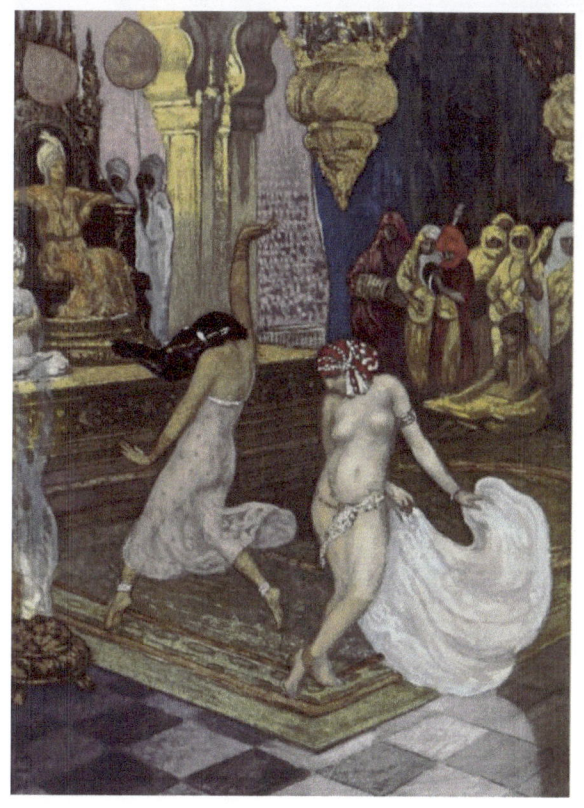

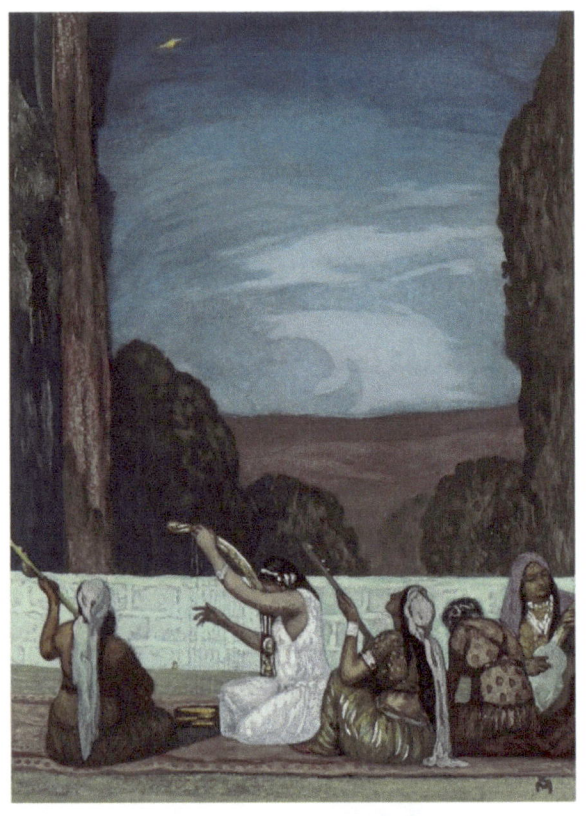

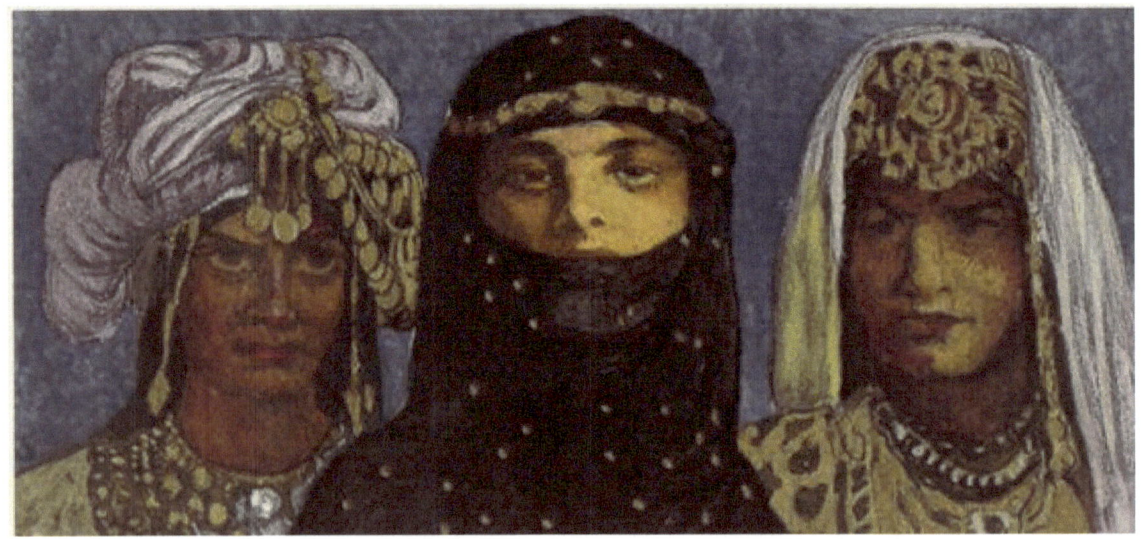

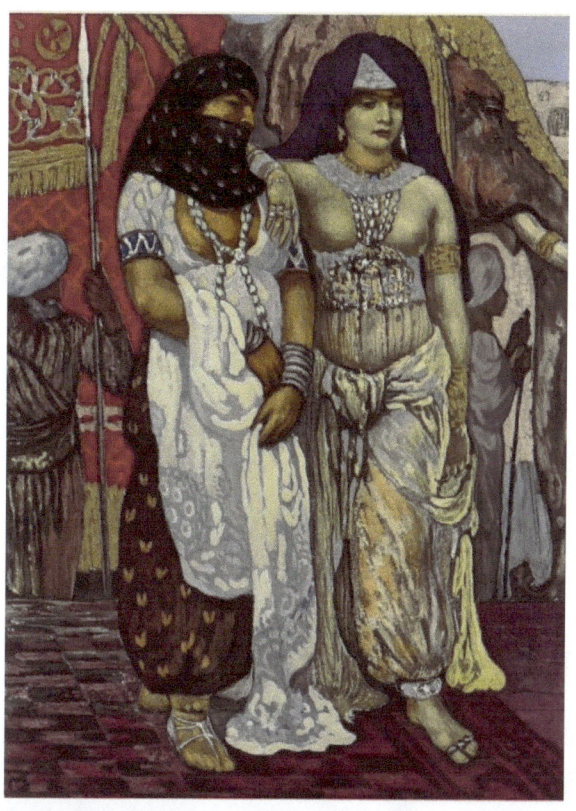

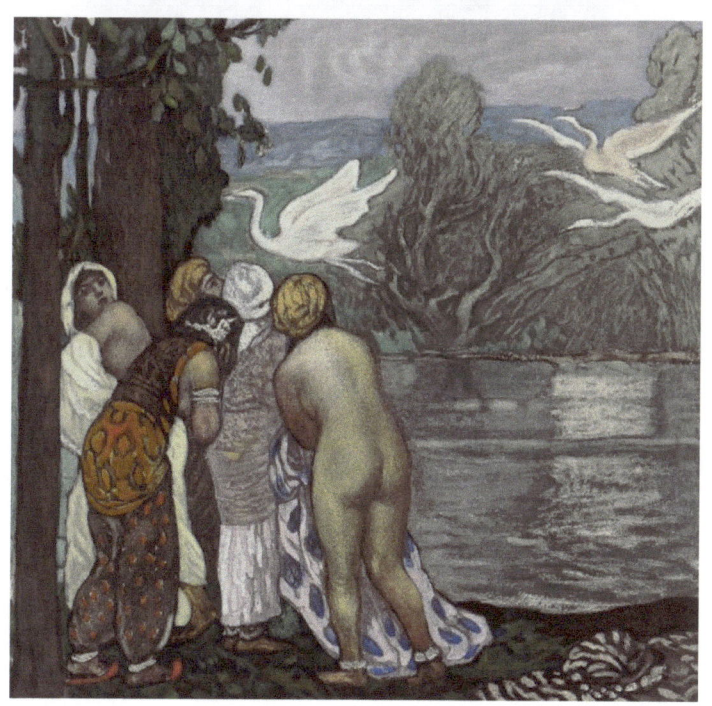

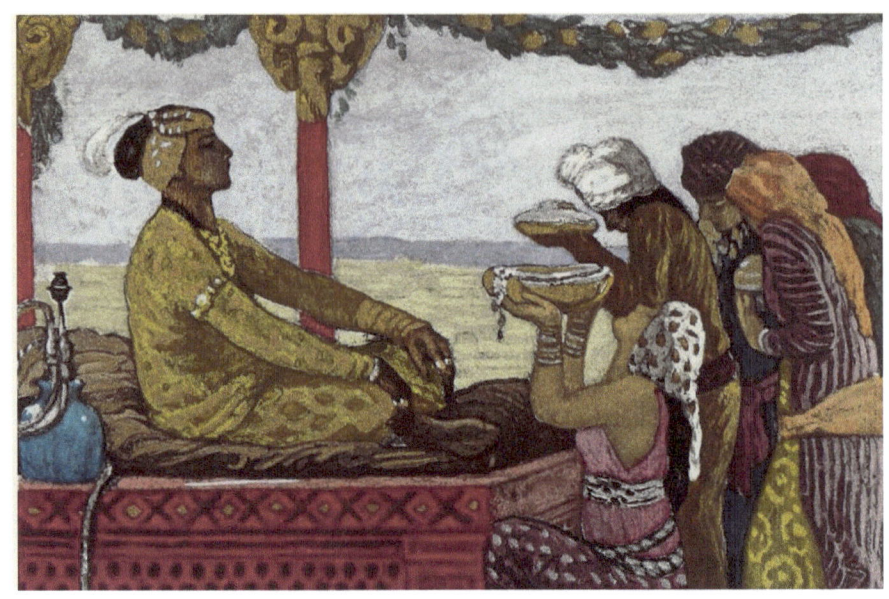

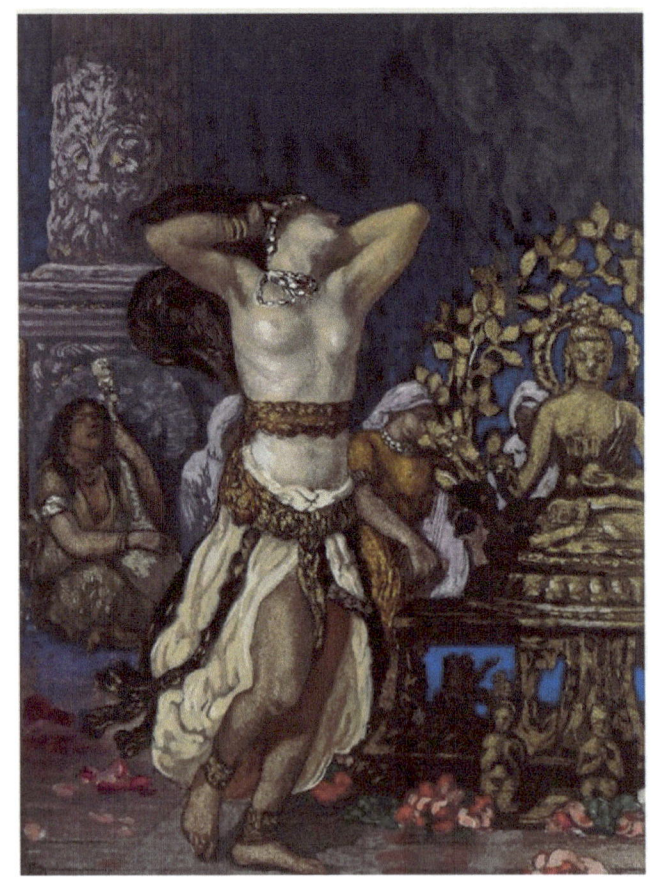

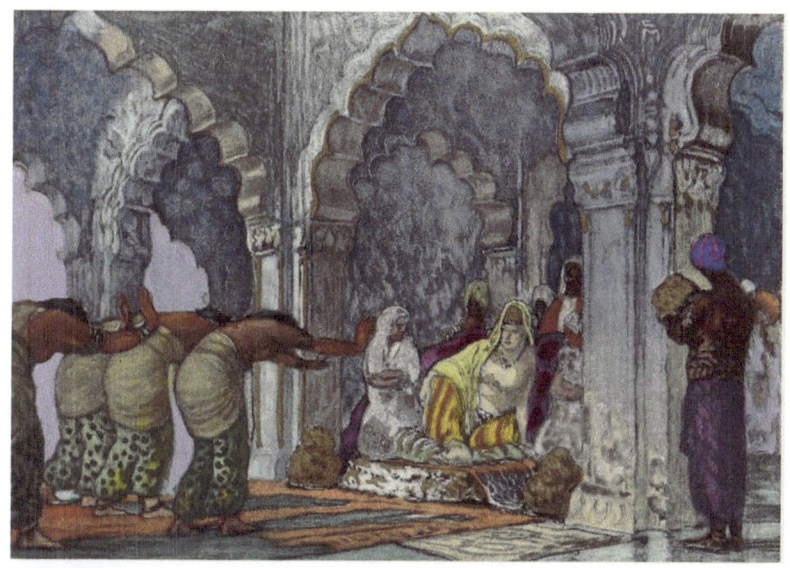

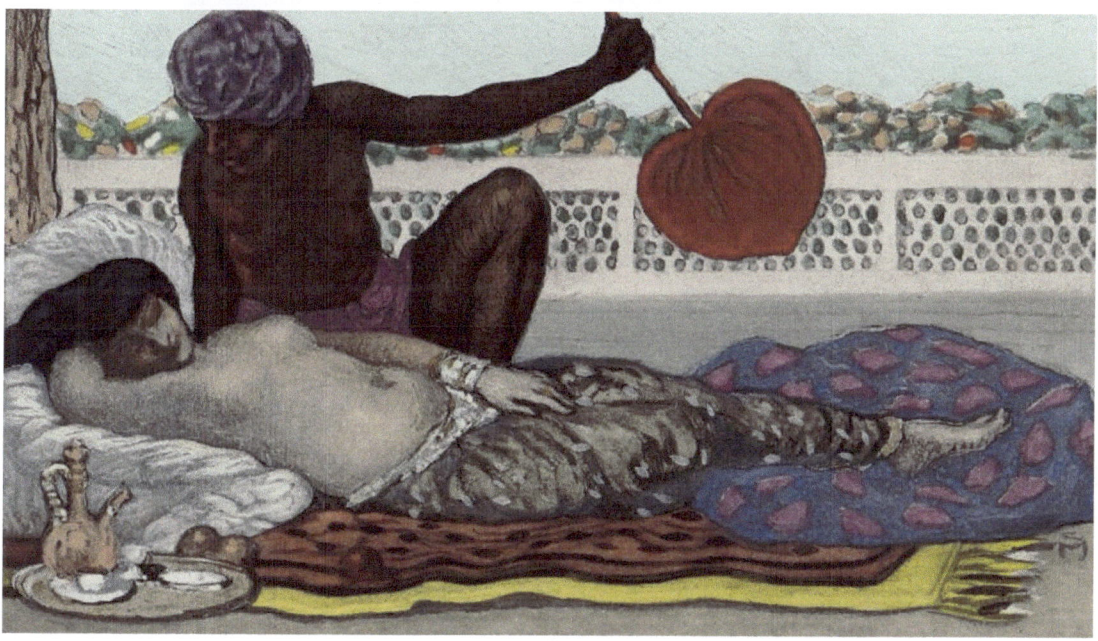

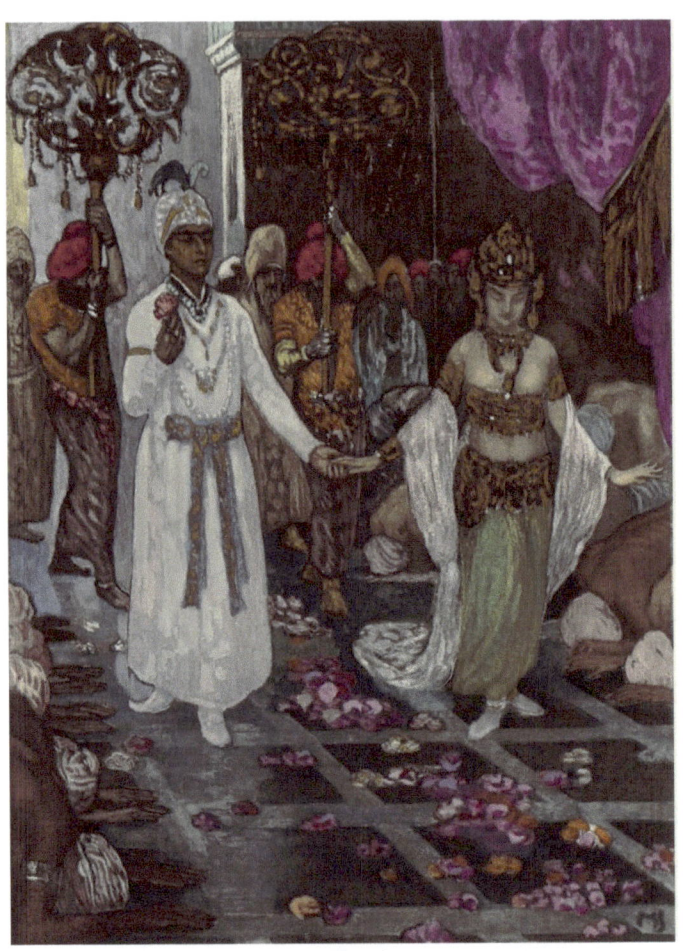

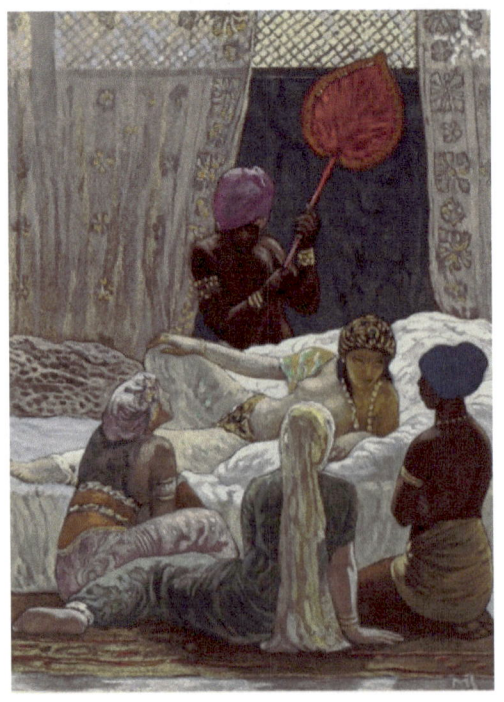

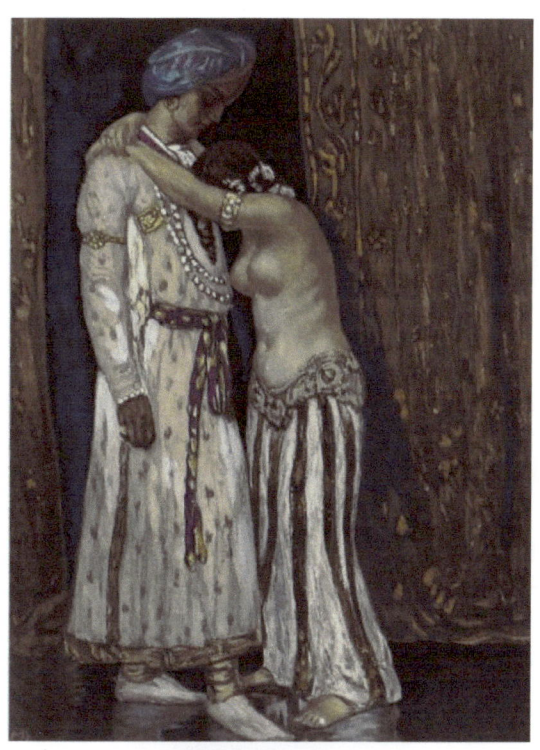

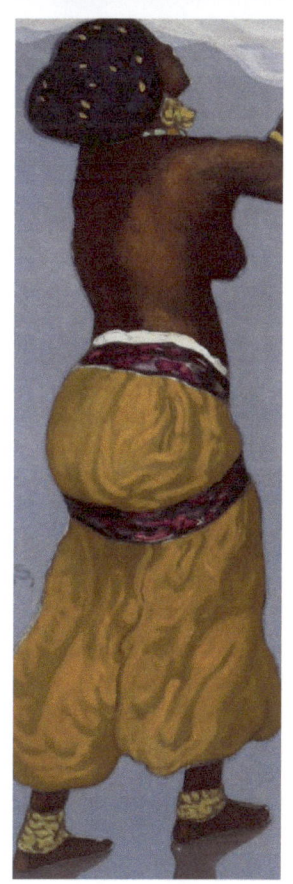